SO WHAT IS CITIZENSHIP ANYWAY?

MERIDIAN MIDDLE SCHOOL
2195 Brandywyn Lane
Buffalo Grove, IL 60089

CHELSEA LUTHRINGER

the rosen publishing group / rosen central

new york

Published in 2000, 2001 by The Rosen Publishing Group, Inc.
29 East 21st Street, New York, NY 10010

Revised Edition 2001

Luthringer, Chelsea.
      So what is citizenship anyway? / Chelsea Luthringer.
         p.   cm.—(A student's guide to American civics)
      Includes bibliographical references and index.
      Summary: Discusses citizenship and how its rights, duties,
and practices affect individuals, groups, and society as a whole.
    ISBN 0-8239-3450-0
    1. Citizenship—United States—Juvenile literature.
[1. Citizenship.] I. Title. II. Series.
JK1759.L86 1999
323.6'0973—dc21   99-23750
                                          CIP

Manufactured in the United States of America

CONTENTS

INTRODUCTION
A GOVERNMENT FOR THE PEOPLE

In your everyday life, you probably have chores and homework. Your parents may tell you to be nice to your little brother or to walk your grandmother to her car after a holiday visit. These are ways in which you participate in your family and community. Did you know that you can also participate in the government?

The government of the United States is a democracy. In a democracy, every citizen is entitled to certain rights and freedoms. An American citizen is a person who was born in the United States or who has chosen to become a member of the United States. In the United States, a citizen's rights and freedoms are guaranteed by the Bill of Rights. The Bill of Rights is made up of the first ten amendments to the U.S. Constitution. The First Amendment, for example, guarantees freedom of speech, freedom of the press, freedom to practice the religion of your choice, and the right to assemble peacefully.

These rights and freedoms have a catch—each citizen who is entitled to them must also uphold them. For a democracy to work properly, every citizen must participate in it. There are many ways to participate. The first way is to become informed of what your rights and responsibilities as an American citizen are.

The Bill of Rights

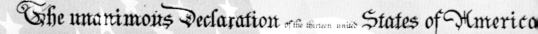

CITIZENSHIP IN THE UNITED STATES

A citizen is a person who is born in a country or who is by choice a member of a nation. A citizen owes loyalty to that nation and is given certain rights by it. Citizenship is the condition of having the rights, privileges, and duties of a citizen.

UNITED STATES INDEPENDENCE

In the 1770s, there were many British subjects living in the American colonies. A subject is a person who owes his or her allegiance, or loyalty, to a king. In this case, the king was George III of England. Many British subjects living in the American colonies did not like or agree with King George. On July 4, 1776, a group of men published the Declaration of Independence. It stated, in part: "These colonies are, of right, and ought to be, free and independent states." The publication of the Declaration of Independence meant that many citizens wanted America to break its ties with England and the king.

The Declaration of Independence   **King George**

CHAPTER ONE

Thomas Jefferson, John Adams, and Benjamin Franklin were members of this group. They and other citizens fought and won the Revolutionary War, the war for America's independence.

From left to right: Benjamin Franklin, John Adams, and Thomas Jefferson

With the publication of the Declaration of Independence, and victory in the war for independence, a new country was born: the United States of America. Along with the new nation came a new kind of citizenship. It was called "citizenship by the consent of the governed." This was a new idea. At that time, there was no other government like it in the world. For the first time, the citizens themselves had a voice in how they would be governed. American citizens still owed allegiance, or loyalty, to the government of the United States, but it would be a government they chose. The citizens had the right to vote for their own government. They could change the government's leadership. All they had to do was exercise their right to vote.

This form of government is also called "government by contract." It was established by the U.S. Constitution, the basis for the nation's laws. Basically, citizens say to their leaders, "We choose you to lead just as you choose to do so. If either of us is ever dissatisfied, the contract is broken. You can stop being a leader anytime you like. If we believe you are not right for the job, on the next election day we can choose someone else." For over two hundred years, the United States has prospered under this new form of government. America's form of democracy has been duplicated in many countries around the world.

Over time, the Constitution required changes and improvements. The right of citizenship needed to be extended to all Americans. Originally, the Constitution did not outlaw slavery. Only men who owned property could vote. The authors of the Constitution provided a system that allowed

Statue of a slave in chains

13TH AMENDMENT
SLAVERY IS OUTLAWED

changes, called amendments, to be made to the document. The federal government amends the Constitution to provide laws for all citizens that are more fair.

The Thirteenth Amendment to the Constitution, added in 1870, outlawed slavery.

The Nineteenth Amendment, added in 1920, gave women the right to vote. Democracy—government by and for the people—continues to be an example to other nations, such as the Philippines, Poland, France, and South Africa. America proves that its citizens are able to govern themselves using elected representatives to speak for them and make laws for the whole nation.

CITIZENSHIP IN THE UNITED STATES
A person can become a citizen of the United States in two ways: by birth or by naturalization.

BIRTH If a person is born in the United States or born in another country to an American parent, he or she is automatically a U.S. citizen.

NATURALIZATION A person can move to the United States from another country and choose to become a U.S. citizen. This is called naturalization. Generally, a person must be eighteen years old to apply for U.S. citizenship.

SOME OF THE REQUIREMENTS FOR CITIZENSHIP ARE:

✔ **Living in the United States as a permanent resident for at least five years**

✔ **Being able to read, write, and speak basic English**

✔ **Understanding the history, principles, and forms of U.S. government**

✔ **Having a moral, or good, character**

People applying for U.S. citizenship must pass a test on U.S. history. Once they pass the test, they must take an oath of allegiance—make a promise to support the Constitution, obey the laws of the United States, give up their allegiance to their native countries, and agree to serve in the armed forces, if necessary.

Can you answer these questions?

Q What is the United States Capitol?

A *The place where Congress meets.*

Q Where is the White House located?

A *Washington, DC.*

Q Name one right guaranteed by the First Amendment.

A *Freedom of speech, freedom of the press, freedom of religion, the right to peaceable assembly, and the right to request change of the government.*

Q Who is the commander in chief of the U.S. military?

A *The president.*

Q Who was the first commander in chief of the U.S. military?

A *George Washington.*

SAMPLE U.S. HISTORY QUESTIONS

Q **In what month do we vote for the president?**

A *November.*

Q **In what month is the new president inaugurated?**

A *January.*

Q **What are the two major political parties in the United States?**

A *Republican and Democratic.*

Q **How many states are there in the United States of America?**

A *Fifty (50).*

Reprinted courtesy of the Immigration and Naturalization Service.

Whether you were born in the United States or chose to become a member of the nation, being a U.S. citizen comes with certain rights and responsibilities. By accepting the responsibilities, citizens can help the democratic government protect their rights.

THE RIGHTS OF A U.S. CITIZEN

Citizens of the United States are entitled to many rights. The Bill of Rights defines and explains these rights.

THERE ARE THREE BASIC KINDS OF RIGHTS: PERSONAL, POLITICAL, AND ECONOMIC.

✔ *Personal rights* allow individuals to express themselves. These rights include the freedom to practice the religion of their choice, the freedom to speak and publish their opinions, and the freedom to move from one location to another.

✔ *Political rights* ensure that citizens may play an active role in their government. These include the right to vote, to

This Boy Scout learns a lot about citizenship with his troop.

so what is citizenship anyway?

gather peacefully, and to petition for change. A petition is a document that states an opinion about a law, policy, or situation along with a request for change. Petitions are signed by a large number of people who agree with the opinion and the requested change.

 Economic rights protect the personal property and finances of a citizen. People own property—homes, cars, and other items—that they earn by working. Governments ensure that no one can take your property by theft or by force. Many laws protect your property rights from a corrupt government, too.

Police officers help enforce the laws.

In addition to these rights, the U.S. government offers its citizens basic protections.

THE U.S. GOVERNMENT MUST PROVIDE THE FOLLOWING FOR ITS CITIZENS:

✔ *Physical safety.* Protecting citizens from enemies within and outside of the United States is part of the government's job. To provide protection, the local, state, and federal, or national, governments establish military and police forces. In times of war, citizens volunteer or are called (drafted) to military service. They serve in the armed forces along with people who make their careers in the service.

✔ *Public services.* These may include building and maintaining roads and bridges, printing money, running schools, and providing public transportation. There are many tasks that affect everyone in the nation. It simply would not work if, for instance, every family created its own form of money. Governments have traditionally done these jobs.

EXERCISING AND DEFENDING YOUR RIGHTS

As U.S. citizens, we enjoy our rights every day. We can say that we like or dislike what the president does without fear of being arrested for our opinions. We can publish just about anything we want in newspapers, flyers, and books. We can buy things without fearing that the government will come and take them away. We can live wherever we want within the United States. Some of these rights were gained over time and after long battles.

Many women, like these, fought for the right to vote.

Women's Right to Vote

Until 1920, women were not allowed to vote in the United States. Many people believed that women were unable to understand politics and the way government worked. Therefore, they thought women were unable to make good decisions about who should be in government. During the middle and late 1800s, thousands of women, called suffragists, used their First Amendment right to write articles, give speeches, and march peacefully to protest this way of thinking. They believed strongly that women, as citizens, had the right to have a say in who represented them in the government. Susan B. Anthony and Elizabeth Cady Stanton were two famous suffragists who fought for women's right to vote. Slowly, they were able to gain support for this right. Finally, in 1920, the Nineteenth Amendment was passed, giving women the right to vote.

The Right to Equal Treatment

Frederick Douglass and Harriet Tubman were two of the best-known advocates for the abolition of slavery. In the United States, slaves had no rights. According to the Constitution, a slave was considered three-fifths of a person— every five slaves were counted as three people. A slave could be bought or sold just like a cow or a house. Slaves had no say in where they lived or whom they worked for.

Susan B. Anthony (left) and Elizabeth Cady Stanton

They had no representation in government. Slaves could not own property and were not allowed to learn or be taught how to read or write.

Frederick Douglass

Frederick Douglass was born into slavery in 1817 in Baltimore, Maryland. Although it was against the law, Douglass learned to read and write. As a young man, Douglass managed to escape to the North, where slavery had been abolished. He became a free man and gave speeches and wrote articles about the horrors of slavery. He started a newspaper devoted to the anti-slavery movement. The northern states went to war against the South in 1861, in part over the issue of slavery. This was the American Civil War. During this war, Frederick Douglass helped set up the first black unit in the Union, or Northern, army. Years later, the North won the Civil War. In 1865, slavery was outlawed by the Thirteenth Amendment to the Constitution. All former slaves became citizens of the United States. They were entitled to the same rights as the people who had once owned them. However, black citizens were not treated as equals by many Americans. Douglass dedicated his life to fighting for equal rights for black people.

Harriet Tubman

Araminta Ross, also known as Harriet Tubman, was born a slave around 1820 on a plantation in the South. As a child, Tubman was forced to work long, grueling hours in her owner's house and in the cotton fields. She was whipped regularly and had little food to eat. In 1849, Tubman made her escape to freedom by traveling on the Underground Railroad. This was a secret route followed by runaway slaves from the South who fled to the North, some as far as Canada. More than 70,000 slaves were freed through the Underground Railroad. Once free, Tubman risked her life and became a "conductor" on the Underground Railroad. She brought more than 300 people to freedom. During the Civil War, Tubman worked as a nurse, a scout, and a spy for the Union army. She fought for women's right to vote, helped raise money for

Many slaves found freedom through the Underground Railroad.

schools for black students, and established a home for elderly black people. Her courage, strength, and devotion to the cause of equal rights is still honored today.

Civil Rights

You probably recognize these names: Martin Luther King Jr., Malcolm X, and Medgar Evers. These great black Americans fought for civil rights in the 1950s and 1960s. Civil rights are the nonpolitical, or private, rights of citizens. These include the right to liberty and to be treated fairly and equally. What you may not realize is that the fight for civil rights continues today.

In 1999, four New York City police officers shot twenty-two-year-old Amadou Diallo forty-one times. They suspected that Diallo was a rapist they were looking for and that he was reaching for a weapon. Diallo

Top: Martin Luther King Jr.
Middle: Malcolm X
Bottom: Medgar Evers

wasn't the rapist, and he didn't have a weapon. The officers were white; Amadou Diallo was black. Many people, such as Reverend Jesse Jackson, believe this was a racial crime. Many people believe that there are often such crimes against people of color. In August 1997, Abner Louima, a Haitian immigrant, was arrested after a fight in New York City. Five police officers were accused of having brutally beaten and abused Louima while he was in custody. Thousands of people protested this alleged abuse.

Police officers were tried, convicted, and sent to jail for the Louima beating, which might not have happened if there had been no public protests. The rights to protest, to march, and to speak out and express differing opinions are guaranteed by the Bill of Rights and are essential to our democratic way of life.

The Reverends Jesse Jackson (left) and Al Sharpton marched to protest the Amadou Diallo shooting.

so what is citizenship anyway?

The Responsibilities of a U.S. Citizen

In a democracy, the people elect the government. We are responsible for what our government does. In a democracy, the people give the orders. If the government does something wrong, the people have the power to change it. This difference is like the difference between owning a bike and renting a bike. If things don't work on the bike, the renter can simply blame the place he or she rented it from. When you own a bike, you are responsible for making sure it works. There is nobody else to blame should the bike break down. To keep things running right, you have to learn how they operate. You must make an effort to keep them in working order.

BE INFORMED

The only way you can know whether the government is working the way you think it should be is to be informed about what and how it's doing. Being informed begins in school. There you learn about the history of the United States. You study the parts of the government and what they do. That gives you the basic information you need. However, a good citizen stays on top of current events, too.

You can learn about current events by reading the newspaper or watching the news on television. You may read about the decision the president

Reading the newspaper is one way to be informed about what's happening in the country.

made to assist another country by sending in armed forces. You might learn about the new tax laws. During election time, you can read about the candidates and the changes they plan to make.

You can also learn by listening to what's going on in your neighborhood. Maybe your next-door neighbors think the corner needs a traffic light. Your parents may not agree with the policies proposed by the board of education in your school district. Somebody is always discussing, debating, or arguing about any issue you can imagine. There are often public meetings and hearings, especially on local issues. These meetings are open to all interested citizens.

Good citizens take the time to listen to these discussions. They read and keep up with current events. Good citizens listen to both sides of arguments. They get their news from more than one source. Only after they are well informed do they make a decision.

VOTE

Once you are informed, it is time to vote for a candidate who will represent your opinions. This happens at many levels. Your school may hold elections for the class president. Local representatives include mayors, members of the town council, and district legislators. State representatives include senators and governors. At the federal

New York City mayor Rudy Giuliani

level, we elect the president. In the United States, the best turnouts—when citizens exercise their voting privileges and cast their votes—are for presidential elections. A citizen must be eighteen years old to vote in a local, state, or federal election. About 60 percent of Americans eligible to vote show up to cast their ballots for president. Voter turnout can be as low as 20 percent for local elections. The reason for this may be the voters' lack of interest in or knowledge of local politics, politicians, and issues.

There are directions inside voting booths to help you.

Decisions that a local government makes usually affect the daily life of a citizen. A local government can have more impact than the federal government. The president of the United States cannot help an individual. He can't order the public works department to fix the potholes in a street or add a stop sign to a dangerous corner. The president can't tell the local board of education to add teachers to a school. The mayor and his or her commissioners can.

Voting is an important responsibility. An election is held whether or not the citizens cast their votes. When large numbers of people do not vote, the power in the government passes to the few who do.

An unworthy candidate, backed by a small, well-organized group, can get many supporters to the polls. A poll is where the votes are cast. Unless many other citizens exercise their right to vote, such a candidate can get elected and hold power for an entire term of office. This may be as short as a year or as long as six years, depending on the office.

OBEY THE LAW

Obeying the law sounds simple and obvious. What most people don't realize is that laws are what keeps a society in order. They are what makes a society work. In the United States, for example, there is one full-time police officer for every 487 citizens. One officer could not force 487 people to obey the law. Citizens are expected to police their own behavior. Most people do. They are taught from childhood to obey the law. The difference between right and wrong is learned so thoroughly that most people feel guilty if they do something wrong, even if no one is watching. Most people would

Police officers protect citizens and enforce the country's laws.

not steal merchandise from a store even if no one was watching and they were certain they could get away with it. Think about how strongly a person must believe in the idea of obeying the law to do that.

PAY TAXES

The government must pay for the services it provides. Its only source of money is the taxes paid by its citizens. Many citizens complain that their taxes are too high, but they are getting a bargain. Suppose your family had to pay for the cost of the roads, bridges, and tunnels leading to your house. You probably couldn't afford it. The job can be done only because the cost is shared. Everyone pays his or her share when he or she pays taxes.

PARTICIPATE IN JURY DUTY

A jury is a group of citizens who hear evidence in a court of law. The jury must then make a decision based on the evidence it has heard. A trial by a jury of one's peers (equals) is a right guaranteed by the Constitution. To preserve this right, citizens must be willing to sit on a jury. That may mean

A jury box is where the jury sits to hear the evidence presented in a trial.

so what is citizenship anyway?

taking time away from family, work, and other activities. It is an important aspect of democracy and a duty that every citizen should be willing to perform, and perform responsibly.

SERVE IN THE ARMED FORCES

This is an important and potentially dangerous duty of a citizen. When the government asks, people put their lives on the line to protect all citizens of the country. Most good citizens think of military service as "the price of freedom." The armed forces include the army, navy, air force, marines, and coast guard.

DO PUBLIC SERVICE

Public service means doing work that helps the community in some way. You can volunteer at the local animal shelter. You can join an environmental group such as the Audubon Society and work toward educating people about preserving the environment. You can offer to help an elderly neighbor clean her apartment or carry her groceries. If you have an interest in music or the performing arts, you can sing or dance for patients in hospitals or nursing homes. You can volunteer in a literacy program and teach people how to read. With the help of an adult volunteer, you can do many things. You and your friends can start a community garden in an empty lot. All of these things help a community become stronger.

By accepting the responsibilities that go along with being a U.S. citizen, we help preserve the democratic ideals on which the United States was based. A democracy works only if the people who live under it participate in it.

This sailor has shown his citizenship by joining the navy.

MAKING A DIFFERENCE

One of the best things that a democracy offers its citizens is the chance to work for something they believe in and to change existing laws. Here are some examples of people who did just that.

A WOMAN'S RIGHT TO CHOOSE

Before 1973, each state decided for itself whether abortion (the termination of a pregnancy) was legal. Many people believe that the choice of whether to carry a fetus to term should be a woman's decision, not the state's. People who believe this are "pro-choice." In 1973, a woman named Norma McCorvey, together with two lawyers, Sarah Weddington and Linda Coffee, won a lawsuit in Texas based on McCorvey's decision to get an abortion. A federal court decided that the choice of whether to end a pregnancy was a woman's constitutional right. This decision was based on the Fourteenth Amendment. It overruled the laws that individual states had passed. Many people disagree with this interpretation of the Fourteenth Amendment. They are anti-abortion, or "pro-life." The pro-choice/pro-life debate continues to this day.

Norma McCorvey (left) and her attorney

CHAPTER FOUR

Dr. Jack Kevorkian as he hears his guilty verdict

EUTHANASIA
EUTHANASIA
EUTHANASIA
EUTHANASIA
EUTHANASIA
EUTHANASIA
EUTHANASIA
EUTHANASIA
EUTHANASIA

THE RIGHT OF EUTHANASIA

Euthanasia is the practice of putting to death, or permitting the putting to death of, a person or animal rather than allowing him or her to suffer through a terminal illness or a lifelong painful condition that cannot be cured. Some people strongly believe in euthanasia. Many people believe that euthanasia is wrong, that every life should be sustained as long as possible. Euthanasia is illegal in all but one state in the United States. Only Oregon has a law that allows a terminally ill patient to request euthanasia.

Seventy-year-old Dr. Jack Kevorkian, sometimes referred to as Dr. Death, believes in euthanasia. He is a retired pathologist—a doctor who treats diseases—who lives in Michigan. Since 1990, he has helped 130 people to kill themselves painlessly. In 1998, Kevorkian videotaped himself giving a fifty-two-year-old man an injection of lethal drugs. The man, Thomas Youk, had Lou Gehrig's disease, a terribly painful and fatal illness that eventually leaves a person unable to speak, swallow, or move. According to Youk's widow and brother, Youk didn't want to live with this disease. Kevorkian delivered a copy of the videotape to CBS's TV news show *60 Minutes,* hoping they would air it. They did. Kevorkian was arrested and convicted for second-degree murder. He received a ten- to twenty-five-year jail sentence for his actions, but he used the trial to tell the public that he believed medically assisted suicide, or patholysis, should be legal.

The state of Oregon legalized assisted suicide in 1997. Since then, forty-three people in Oregon legally committed suicide with the help of their doctors. Some people hope that other states will join Oregon. Many hope they will not. It is up to the citizens of the United States to fight for what they want as the law in their state.

so what is citizenship anyway?

EQUAL RIGHTS IN ATHLETICS

In 1972, Congress passed Title IX, an amendment to the Civil Rights Act. Title IX, which went into effect in 1978, requires all schools that receive money from the federal government for sports programs to provide equal funding for women's and men's sports. At that time, few, if any, high schools or colleges offered sports for women. Afterward, if a school refused to comply, it would lose its federal funding. Before Title IX, only one in twenty-seven girls competed in high school sports. Today, one in three does.

The law was passed because of the efforts of Bernice Resnick Sandler and hundreds of other women. Sandler organized a campaign to end discrimination against women in federally funded schools. Among other strategies, Sandler persuaded hundreds of women to write to their representatives in the House of Representatives and the Senate about the issue. It was, in part, because of the outcry of these women that Congress passed Title IX.

High school and college students across the United States help to ensure that schools obey the law of Title IX. In 1994, a group of female athletes at Brown University sued their school for trying to drop four women's sports. The court ruled in favor of the female athletes in 1997. Fearing similar lawsuits, many other universities began to comply with Title IX guidelines. Students helped make a difference. You can, too.

As a result of protest, today there are many opportunities for girls to participate in sports.

so what is citizenship anyway?

What's Next?

Being a U.S. citizen is a privilege and a responsibility. As a citizen, you have the right to voice your opinions. You also have the responsibility to speak up if you don't agree with the way things are run. These rights and responsibilities go hand in hand with being a U.S. citizen.

You can be a good citizen by keeping informed about a variety of issues that may affect you, your family, and your community. Such issues often involve state or national government matters such as road or highway construction, taxes, and sometimes even international affairs. Other concerns may affect you more personally, such as your local government's law enforcement and protection responsibilities.

Watch the news, read the newspaper, and discuss today's issues with your parents, friends, and teachers. When you turn eighteen, you will be allowed to vote. You will help choose the people who run our country. You need to be informed to make smart choices.

Look around for ways you can help in your community. Volunteer to help clean up the neighborhood park. Work in a soup kitchen two Saturdays a month. Help organize a petition for a needed service or government project like a stop sign or traffic light at a busy intersection.

Good citizens help their communities. This boy is helping to clean the local park.

so what is citizenship anyway?

All of these services are needed but often are not performed by busy and underfunded government agencies. Volunteers create opportunity for other citizens. These volunteer efforts are greatly appreciated by those who benefit from the many completed volunteer projects.

Good citizens care about their country, community, and other citizens. They are willing to work hard to make things better for everyone. You can help to make the world better. You know your rights and responsibilities. It's up to you to do something about them.

The Statue of Liberty is a symbol of freedom to foreigners seeking citizenship in the United States.

GLOSSARY

advocate A person who publicly supports something.

allegiance Devotion to something or someone.

amendment A change to something.

Bill of Rights The first ten amendments to the U.S. Constitution.

citizen A person who by birth or choice is a member of a nation.

civil rights The nonpolitical rights of every citizen of the United States, of whatever race, color, religion, or sex.

constitution A document stating a government's powers.

current events Things that are happening in the present time.

debate A discussion of reasons for and against something.

democracy A government that is run by the people who live under it.

election A selection by vote.

inaugurate To officially place into office the winning candidate of an election.

jury A group of citizens selected to hear evidence in a case brought before a court of law.

loyalty A feeling or the behavior of being true and faithful to something or someone.

naturalization The process by which a person from one country is granted citizenship in another country.

peer A person who is the equal of another person.

poll A place where votes are cast or recorded.

protest A statement or act in which a person or group objects strongly to something.

representative A person who is appointed or elected to act or speak for others.

responsibility A sense of duty or the obligation to take care of something or someone.

right Something to which a person is entitled.

slavery The practice of owning other people.

subject A person who owes his or her loyalty to a king or queen.

suffragist A person who fights for the right to vote.

volunteer To offer your services for free.

FOR FURTHER READING

Atgwa, Paul, et al., eds. *Stand Up for Your Rights*. Chicago: World Book, Inc., 1998.

Bratman, Fred. *Becoming a Citizen: Adopting a New Home*. Austin, TX: Raintree/Steck-Vaughn, 1993.

Heath, David. *Elections in the United States*. Mankato, MN: Capstone Press, 1999.

O'Connor, Maureen. *Equal Rights*. Danbury, CT: Franklin Watts, Inc., 1998.

Shuker-Haines, Frances. *Rights and Responsibilities*. Austin, TX: Raintree/Steck-Vaughn, 1993.

Weizmann, Daniel. *Take a Stand! Everything You Never Wanted to Know About Government*. Los Angeles: Price, Stern, Sloan Publishers, 1996.

RESOURCES

BOY SCOUTS OF AMERICA

Contact the Boy Scouts of America council in your area.
Web site:
http://www.bsa.scouting.org/

DO SOMETHING

423 West 55th Street
8th Floor
New York, NY 10019
(212) 523-1175
Web site:
http://www.dosomething.org/

GIRL SCOUTS OF AMERICA

Contact the Girl Scouts of America council in your area.
Web site:
http://www.girlscouts.org/

WEB SITES

Democracy in Action
http://tqjunior.advanced.org/4410

Girls Incorporated
http://www.girlsinc.org

Teens Newsweek
http://www.weeklyreader.com/teennewsweek

Time for Kids
http://www.pathfinder.com/tfk

INDEX

ABOUT THE AUTHOR

Chelsea Luthringer is a freelance writer in New York. She is the author of two Rosen Central books for young adults.

PHOTO CREDITS

Cover photo by Thaddeus Harden; pp. 5, 8, 18, 20, 21, 22, 29, © Corbis/Bettman; pp. 6, 19 © Corbis; p. 7 © Corbis/Archivo Iconografico, S.A.; p. 8 © Corbis/North Carolina Museum of Art; pp. 15, 38 © Skjold; p. 16 by Kelly Hahn; p. 22 © Corbis/Flip Schulke; pp. 23, 34 © Corbis/AFP; p. 24 by Thaddeus Harden; p. 26 © Corbis/Mitchell Gerber; p. 27 © Corbis/Joseph Sohm, ChromoSohm, Inc.; p. 28 © Corbis/Adamsmith Productions; p. 30 © TonyStone/Phil Schofield; p. 40–41 © Corbis/Kit Kittle.

Design and Layout
Kim M. Sonsky

Consulting Editors
Mark Beyer and Jennifer Ceaser